D1627955

A CHILD'S GUIDE TO THE BBC MICRO

John Dewhirst

CAMBRIDGE UNIVERSITY PRESS
Cambridge
London   New York   New Rochelle
Melbourne   Sydney

Published by the Press Syndicate of the University of Cambridge
The Pitt Building, Trumpington Street, Cambridge CB2 1RP.
32 East 57th Street, New York, NY 10022, USA.
296 Beaconsfield Parade, Middle Park, Melbourne 3206, Australia.

© Cambridge University Press 1983

First published 1983

British Library cataloguing in publication data
Dewhirst, John
A childs guide to the BBC Micro
1. BBC Microcomputer
I.Title
001.64'04   QA76.8.B3

ISBN 0 521 27731 0 Schools Edition
ISBN 0 521 27730 2 Family Edition

Produced by Chancerel Publishers Ltd, 40 Tavistock Street,
London WC2.
Printouts by Technology for Business Ltd, 157 Farringdon Road,
London EC1.
Typesetting and Graphic Reproduction by ReproSharp Ltd, 47 Farringdon
Road, London EC1
Printed by Richard Clay (The Chaucer Press) Ltd, Bungay, Suffolk, England.

CONTENTS

INTRODUCTION

Each section of the book is written by a different person. Each person is an expert at their job and gives very useful advice. Read their advice very carefully. The advice is given at the start of their section of the book. If you follow the advice it will make the work you do much easier.

SECTIONS

1. The keyboard by Pru Comet – typist.
Miss Comet shows you the ways in which the various types of keys work and the position of the keys on the keyboard.

2. Getting started by P. C. Truemo – investigator.
P. C. Truemo shows you how to get started on the computer, how to make it print numbers and words, calculate answers and finally store items in its memory.

3. Special features by Mort Puce – artist.
Mort Puce shows you how to draw coloured pictures on the screen and to make the computer play music.

4. Writing programs by Prof. O. Crumpet – designer.
Professor O. Crumpet shows you how to copy, adapt, then finally design your own programs.

5. Finding out by Miss O. C. Termup – librarian.
Miss O. C. Termup shows you how to use the six different reference sections.

Mep Court,
Portcume.

Dear Reader,

Hello there. We are the people who have written this book and you will find out more about us as you read through it. When you meet us we shall introduce ourselves.

The book has been written for people who know nothing about computers, but who want to find out for themselves. It has been written to show you not just what the computer can do, but more importantly, what *you* can make the computer do for you.

We have put together all our good ideas so that it is easy for you to find out just how the BBC microcomputer works. The book is written in five sections and we have each written a section. The first four sections are to be read and worked through in order, but the last section is for reference and this can be used at any time for checking.

Happy computing!

Prudence Comet

Bobby Truemo

Mortimer Puce

Oliver Crumpet

Olive Constance Termup

In each section of the book you will come across different types of diagrams. The things for you to try, that is various exercises and experiments, will all be given a 'You try' box.

The 'You try' box looks like this.

```
┌─────────────────────────┐
│                         │
└─────────────────────────┘
```

You try

```
┌─────────────────────────┐
│                         │
└─────────────────────────┘
```

The things which are displayed on the screen will all be shown in a 'Display' box. The 'Display' box looks like this.

The things which you need to make a note about and remember will all be given in a 'Make a note' box. The 'Make a note' box looks like this.

THE KEYBOARD

Pru Comet

My advice

Don't be afraid of the computer. I think of it as a typewriter with a difference. Try things out. In this way you will learn quickly just what it can and cannot do. When you try things out, the computer will send messages back to you. This is the way the computer talks to you. It can make noises, change colours on the screen and do lots of other things, so you'll need a bit of time to learn about everything the computer can do. Your first job is to learn about the keyboard, find out where all the keys are and what they all do. A good idea is to make your own notes in a book of all the things you find out about the computer.

As you read through the keyboard section of the book, try things out as you go along. Don't be put off by any messages the computer sends to you. It does not realise that you are a beginner and just trying out a few things for yourself. As you work through the rest of the book you will learn the language that the computer understands, but like learning any language you can only learn a bit at a time.

Pru Comet

There are 74 keys on the BBC microcomputer and the keys can be divided into the following 6 groups:

Control keys	Edit keys
Number keys	Symbol keys
Letter keys	Function keys

But before you start looking at the keys in detail there are a few things you need to know.

1. If you keep your finger on a key it will repeat itself and instead of A you will get AAAAAAAA.

2. You can use ⌈DELETE⌋ as a rub out key. That is, by touching ⌈DELETE⌋ any unwanted characters can be removed. But beware, this key works like all the others and if you keep your finger on it you could rub out more than you intended.

3. If the computer continues to go over something again and again and you want to escape from this then press ⌈ESCAPE⌋ .

Control keys

These are 11 keys which have names on them.

⌈BREAK⌋	⌈SHIFT⌋ (2 keys)
⌈ESCAPE⌋	⌈SHIFT LOCK⌋
⌈RETURN⌋	⌈CAPS LOCK⌋
⌈TAB⌋	⌈CTRL⌋
⌈DELETE⌋	⌈SPACE BAR⌋

BBC User Guide 15

BREAK resets the computer to:

```
BBC Computer
BASIC
>_
```

To make a new start,
BREAK plays the part.

ESCAPE interrupts the computer to:

```
Escape
>_
```

RETURN moves the cursor to the start of the next line. The cursor is a flashing dash or square which shows you where the next character you type will appear on the screen.

TAB moves the cursor one space to the right.

DELETE rubs out the character to the left of the cursor.

SHIFT If this key is held down, the letter keys print capitals and the symbol keys print the upper symbol on the key.

SHIFT LOCK If this has been pressed it is like having SHIFT held down all the time. (A red light below shift lock lights up when it is in use.)

CAPS LOCK When this has been pressed the letter keys print capitals and the symbol keys print the lower symbol or number. (A red light below caps lock lights up when this is in use.) When the machine is first switched on it has the caps lock on.

CTRL The control key (when held down) operates controls.

SPACE BAR This is the long key at the bottom of the keyboard. It is not named like the other keys. It puts in a space.

This is what will appear on the screen.

You try

Press the SPACE BAR (long key) carefully three times.

```
BBC Computer
BASIC
> ─
```

Wrong sort of space bar!

This is what will appear on the screen

You try

Press the SPACE BAR until the cursor goes onto the next line.

```
BBC Computer
BASIC
>
─
```

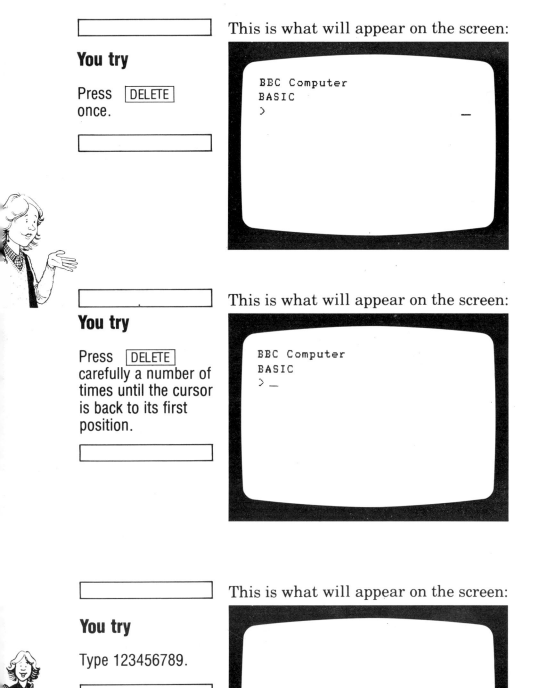

You try

Press DELETE once.

This is what will appear on the screen:

```
BBC Computer
BASIC
>                              _
```

You try

Press DELETE carefully a number of times until the cursor is back to its first position.

This is what will appear on the screen:

```
BBC Computer
BASIC
> _
```

You try

Type 123456789.

This is what will appear on the screen:

```
> 123456789_
```

This is what will appear on the screer

You try

Press [DELETE]
nine times.

Make a note

Each time [DELETE]
is pressed the cursor
moves one place to
the left and rubs out
any letter or number
which is there.

>_

This is what will appear on the scree

You try

Type QWERTY.

>QWERTY _

This is what will appear on the scree

You try

Press [DELETE] six
times.

>_

You try

Press the SPACE BAR and do not release it until the cursor stops and a note sounds.

This is what will appear on the screen:

```
BBC Computer
BASIC
>
```

Make a note

Each time SPACE BAR is pressed the cursor moves one space to the right. TAB has a similar effect.

You try

Press any letter or number key. The note sounds, but nothing appears on the screen and the computer seems to be jammed. Press ESCAPE .

This is what will appear on the screen:

```
BBC Computer
BASIC
>

Escape
>_
```

Make a note

ESCAPE is used to escape from a situation or routine.

You try

Press BREAK .

This is what will appear on the screen

```
BBC Computer
BASIC
> _
```

Make a note

BREAK resets the computer. (It is like an on/off switch.)

You try

Press RETURN
three times.

This is what will appear on the screen:

```
BBC Computer
BASIC
>
>
>
>_
```

Make a note

RETURN moves the cursor to the next line.

You try

Press BREAK ,
then hold down
CTRL and press
J .

This is what will appear on the screen:

```
BBC Computer
BASIC
>
 _
```

Make a note

CTRL J moves the cursor down a line.

14

BBC User Guide 16

You try

Press BREAK then hold down CTRL and press H .

This is what will appear on the screen:

```
BBC Computer
BASIC
>
```

Make a note

CTRL H moves the cursor one space left.
CTRL I moves the cursor one space right.

Number keys

These are the ten keys which print the numbers 1, 2, 3, 4, 5, 6, 7, 8, 9, Ø.
On the keyboard they are set out in a line
1 2 3 4 5 6 7 8 9 Ø
(The Ø key is used for 0 so that it is not confused with the letter O).

You try

Type out these figures. Press RETURN at the end of each line.	1
	121
	1331
	14641

Letter keys

These are the 26 keys which print the letters of the alphabet.
A, B, C, D, E, F, G, H, I, J, K, L, M, N, O, P, Q, R, S, T, U, V, W, X, Y, Z
and
a, b, c, d, e, f, g, h, i, j, k, l, m, n, o, p, q, r, s, t, u, v, w, x, y, z
On the keyboard they are set out in capitals as

Q W E R T Y U I O P
A S D F G H J K L
Z X C V B N M

which is exactly the same as you would find them on a typewriter.

BBC User Guide 1

You try

Type out the following. Press RETURN at the end of each line.
1ST ROW   QWERTYUIOP
2ND ROW   ASDFGHJKL
3RD ROW   ZXCVBNM

You try

Type out the names of the members of your family and their birthdays. Press RETURN at the end of each line.

You try

Type out:
I can use the keyboard.
Press RETURN .

If you do not like the computer saying 'Mistake' then put a number at the beginning of the line.

Edit keys

Keys light brown, Copy things down.

All the five edit keys are in a lighter brown colour. Four of the keys have arrow signs which point up, down, right and left. The other edit key is [COPY].

BBC User Guide 29

BBC microcomputer
BREAK
ESCAPE 1 2 3 4 5 6 7 8 9 Ø − ^ \
TAB Q W E R T Y U I O P @ [_
CAPS LOCK CTRL A S D F G H J K L ; :] RETURN
SHIFT LOCK SHIFT Z X C V B N M , . / SHIFT DELETE COPY
cassette motor
caps lock
shift lock

The arrow keys move the copying line of the cursor one space in the direction of the arrow pressed. By using these keys the copying line of the cursor can be moved to any position on the screen.

This is what will appear on the screen:

BBC Computer
BASIC
>

You try

Press [BREAK] and then press the up arrow key 4 times, (it looks like this [↑]). Press the left arrow key once (it looks like this [←]).

You try

Press COPY
12 times.

This is what will appear on the screen:

```
BBC Computer __
BASIC
>BBC Computer ■
```

You have used the edit keys to copy a word that is on the screen.

You try

Press ESCAPE .

This is what will appear on the screen:

```
Escape
>_
```

You try

Press the up arrow key once. (This key looks like this ↑.)
Press the left arrow key once. (This key looks like this ←.)

This is what will appear on the screen:

```
Escape
>■
```

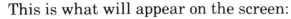

You try

Press COPY six times.

Make a note

The edit keys are used to copy words from the screen.

This is what will appear on the screen:

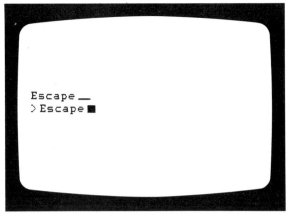

```
Escape _
> Escape ■
```

You try

Press ESCAPE
Then use the edit keys to copy the following words:
cape ape cap ace peas peace

This is what will appear on the screen:

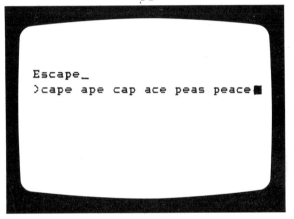

```
Escape_
>cape ape cap ace peas peace■
```

Symbol keys

These are the 12 keys which print symbols and are grouped together on the right hand side of the keyboard. There are also some more symbol keys which are above the number keys and to use these SHIFT must be held down.

You try

Type out the following. Press RETURN at the end of each line.
1 !
2 "
3 #
4 $
5 %
6 &
7 '
8 (
9)

You try

Type out the following. Press RETURN at the end of each line.
1 PUNCTUATION ! " ' ; : , . ?
2 ARITHMETIC % ( ) + − * /
3 OTHER $ & @ £

Find all the keys,
And type with ease.

Function keys

These ten keys are orange in colour and are in a line along the top of the keyboard. There are $f_0, f_1, f_2, f_3, f_4, f_5, f_6, f_7, f_8, f_9$. The keys can be made to do various things and are sometimes called programmable keys.

BBC User Guide 141

These keys can be used to print out a required word, for example the word MAGIC.

You try

Type *KEY Ø MAGIC then press RETURN .

This is what will appear on the screen:

```
>*KEY 0 MAGIC
>_
```

21

You try

Press fø .

This is what will appear on the screen:

```
>MAGIC _
```

Make a note

The function keys can be used to print words on the screen.

Now press
RETURN
to start a new line.

You try

Type
*KEY 1 HER FAT
then press
RETURN .

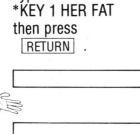

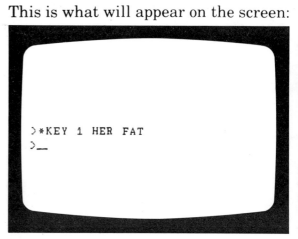

This is what will appear on the screen:

```
>*KEY 1 HER FAT
>_
```

You try

Press f₁ Try holding down
f₁ .

You try

Use the same idea to get the function keys to print out some of your own words.

GETTING STARTED

P. C. Truemo

My advice

When you start to make the computer do things for you always check them very carefully. The computer is very exact in the way it understands things. A missing comma, a full stop in the wrong place or a wrong letter will result in the computer not understanding you.

When this happens – INVESTIGATE – track down every possible mistake until you get everything correct. It may take some time at first to track down your mistakes, but gradually you will not only become quicker at doing this, but you will also make fewer mistakes.

Make notes of the things you find useful, so that you can use them again easily whenever you want. Finally I find these points very useful.

1. Remember that the computer needs all its instructions in CAPITAL letters.

2. Remember that after every instruction you must press RETURN .

Bobby Truemo

Bobby Truemo

In this section you will be shown how to use the computer in four different ways.

1 Using the computer as a typewriter.

You will be shown how to PRINT numbers and characters on the screen and how to space them out in various ways.

2 Using the computer as a calculator.

You will be shown how to add, take away, multiply and divide numbers using the computer.

3 Using the computer for storing information.

You will be shown how to put numbers into the memory of the computer.

4 Using the computer to ask for information.

You will be shown how to get the computer to ask for information, which it then puts into its memory.

When switched on the BBC microcomputer will display the following.

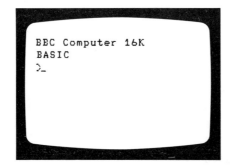

Model A

Model B

Model B with disc drive

BBC Computer – the name of the computer.

16K or 32K – the size of the computer's memory.

Acorn DFS – indicates that a disc drive can be fitted to the computer.

BASIC – the computer language used by the BBC computer.

> This sign is called a prompt. It is the way the computer tells you that it is ready to accept your instructions.

− This sign is called the cursor. So that you do not confuse it with any other sign it flashes on and off.
The cursor normally moves to the right, but it moves to the left and rubs out if ⎡DELETE⎤ is pressed.

The computer as a typewriter   BBC User Guide 324

To make the computer write things we use PRINT.
PRINT must be typed in capital letters and after the statement is complete ⎡RETURN⎤ should be pressed.

Printing numbers

This is what will appear on the screen:

You try

Type PRINT 5 then press ⎡RETURN⎤ .

```
>PRINT 5
           5
> _
```

Make a note

To PRINT a number type PRINT followed by the number and then press ⎡RETURN⎤.

*At the end of a line,
Press RETURN, that's fine.*

You try

Type PRINT 675 then press RETURN .

You try

Using the same idea PRINT some numbers of your own.

[   ]

This is what will appear on the screen:

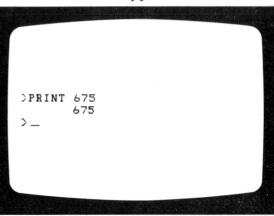

```
>PRINT 675
        675
> _
```

Printing symbols, letters and words

[   ]

This is what will appear on the screen:

You try

Type PRINT "?" then press RETURN .

[   ]

```
>PRINT "?"
?
> _
```

Make a note

To PRINT a symbol, letter or word type PRINT followed by the symbol, letter or word inside speech marks, then press RETURN .

You try

Type PRINT "BEE"
then press RETURN .

This is what will appear on the screen:

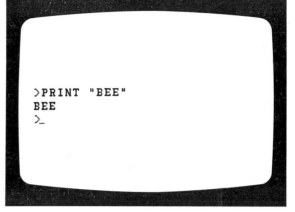

You try

Use PRINT to make
the computer write
your name.

Spacing numbers

You try

Type PRINT 1,2,3,4
then press RETURN .

This is what will appear on the screen:

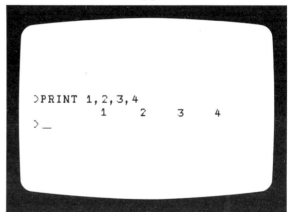

You try

Type PRINT 1;2;3;4
then press RETURN .

This is what will appear on the screen:

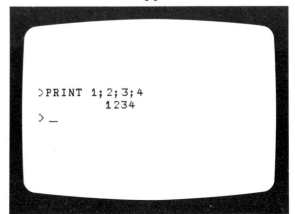

This is what will appear on the screen

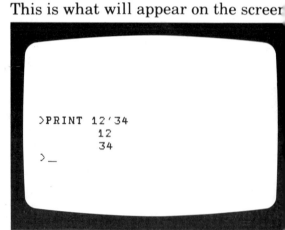

```
>PRINT 12'34
        12
        34
>_
```

You try

Using the same ideas
space out some
numbers of your
own.

Make a note

The symbol
, prints spaced out
; prints without
   spaces
' prints on two lines

Don't stand and wait,
INVESTIGATE.

Spacing words

You try

Type PRINT
"DOG","CAT" then
press RETURN .

This is what will appear on the screen

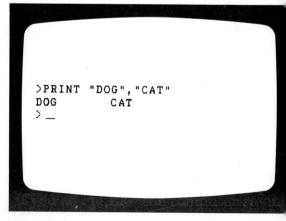

```
>PRINT "DOG","CAT"
DOG        CAT
>_
```

You try

Type PRINT "DOG";"CAT" then press RETURN .

This is what will appear on the screen:

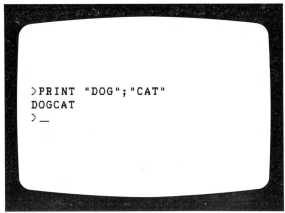

```
>PRINT "DOG";"CAT"
DOGCAT
>_
```

You try

Type PRINT "DOG"'"CAT" then press RETURN .

This is what will appear on the screen:

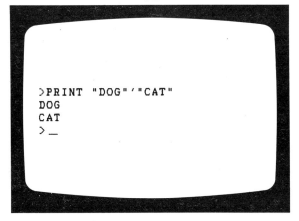

```
>PRINT "DOG"'"CAT"
DOG
CAT
>_
```

You try

Using the same idea space out your first and second names.

Make a note

The symbol
, prints words spaced out
; prints words without spaces
' prints words on two lines

The computer as a calculator

The PRINT statement can also be used to make the computer act like a calculator. It can be given a question and it will supply the answer. Remember that PRINT must be typed in capital letters and after the statement is complete RETURN should be pressed.

This is what will appear on the screen:

You try

Type PRINT 5+7
then press RETURN .

```
>PRINT 5+7
          12
>_
```

Nearly always better,
With CAPITAL letter.

This is what will appear on the screen:

You try

Type PRINT 8−4
then press RETURN .

```
>PRINT 8-4
          4
>_
```

You try

Type PRINT 7*3 then press RETURN .

This is what will appear on the screen:

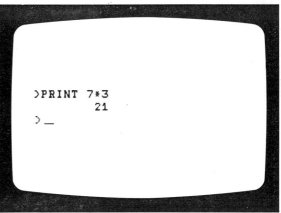

```
>PRINT 7*3
        21
>_
```

You try

Type PRINT 8/4 then press RETURN .

This is what will appear on the screen:

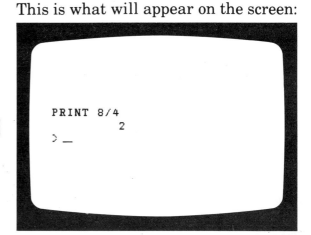

```
PRINT 8/4
         2
>_
```

You try

1. Using the same idea make up some of your own sums.
2. Check a shopping bill with the computer.

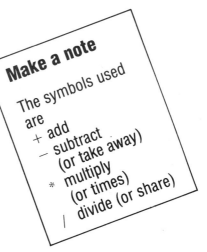

Make a note

The symbols used are

+ add
− subtract (or take away)
* multiply (or times)
| divide (or share)

31

The computer memory

You can also use the computer to remember information. It is important to know just how the computer does this before you go on to the next part of this section.

Just as you live at one address, your friend at another, your teacher at yet another address, so the computer uses a similar system of addresses for storing information.

It stores numbers at the following addresses in its memory. The addresses can either be letters or words. For example

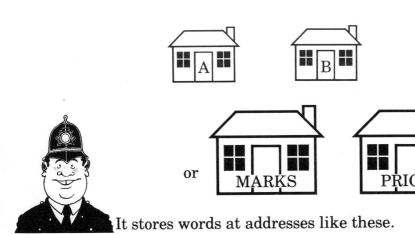

or

It stores words at addresses like these.

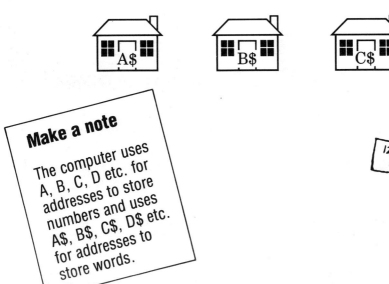

Make a note

The computer uses A, B, C, D etc. for addresses to store numbers and uses A$, B$, C$, D$ etc. for addresses to store words.

Using the computer for storing information

The LET statement is used to put numbers or words into the memory of the computer. LET must be in capital letters.

This is what will appear on the screen:

You try

Type LET A=123
then press RETURN .

```
>LET A=123
>
```

This is what will appear on the screen:

You try

Type PRINT A then
press RETURN .

```
>PRINT A
        123
>_
```

LET A=123 put the number 123 into the memory of the computer at address A. PRINT A recalled the number which was in the memory of the computer at address A.

You try

Using the LET statement put the number 12 into address B and number 4 into address C. Then type PRINT B+C'B−C'B*C'B/C.

33

You try

Type
LET A$="GOOD"
then press RETURN .

This is what will appear on the screen:

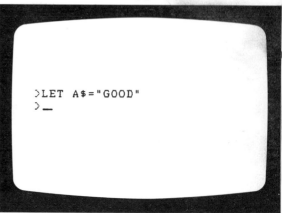

```
>LET A$="GOOD"
>_
```

You try

Type PRINT A$ then
press RETURN .

This is what will appear on the screen:

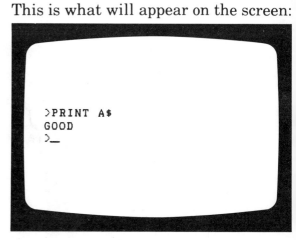

```
>PRINT A$
GOOD
>_
```

LET A$="GOOD" put the word GOOD into the memory of
the computer at address A$. PRINT A$ recalled the word
which was in the memory of the computer at address A$.

You try

Use the LET
statement to put "I"
in the address B$
and "AM" in the
address C$. Type

PRINT C$,B$,A$ and
press RETURN .
Type PRINT B$,C$,A$
then press RETURN .

Using the computer to ask for information

The INPUT statement is used to make the computer ask for numbers or words which it then puts into a memory address. INPUT must be in capital letters.

You try

Type INPUT A then press RETURN .

This is what will appear on the screen:

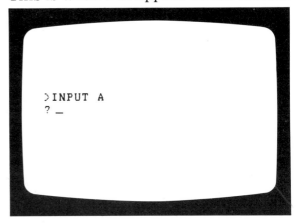

```
>INPUT A
? _
```

You try

Type 99 then press RETURN .

This is what will appear on the screen:

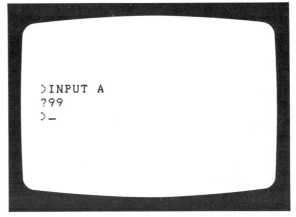

```
>INPUT A
?99
> _
```

You try

Type PRINT A then press RETURN .

This is what will appear on the screen:

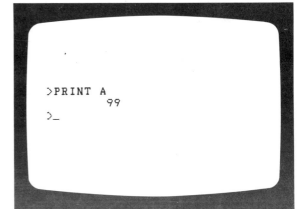

```
>PRINT A
        99
> _
```

INPUT A made the computer ask for a number. When the number 99 was typed, the computer put 99 into the memory address A. PRINT A recalled the number which was in the memory of the computer at address A.

You try

Use the INPUT statement to make the computer ask for some numbers to put into the computer memory addresses B and C. (? is asking for a number). Type PRINT B,C,B+C,B*C.

Make a note

1. INPUT A makes the computer ask for a number.
2. The ? sign is the way the computer asks for a number.
3. The number the computer is given goes into the memory address A.

You try

Type INPUT A$ then press RETURN .

If in doubt,
Try things out.

This is what will appear on the screen:

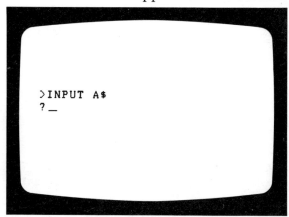

```
>INPUT A$
? _
```

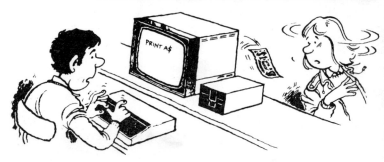

You try

Type HELLO then
press   RETURN .

This is what will appear on the screen:

```
>INPUT A$
?HELLO
> _
```

You try

Type PRINT A$ then
press   RETURN .

This is what will appear on the screen:

```
>PRINT A$
HELLO
> _
```

*What the computer can do,
Is just up to you.*

INPUT A$ made the computer ask for a word. When the
word HELLO was typed in, the computer put HELLO into
the memory address A$. PRINT A$ recalled the word
which was in the memory address A$.

You try

Use the INPUT
statement to put
your name into the
address B$. (? is
asking for a word.)
Type PRINT A$,B$.

Make a note

1. INPUT A$ makes
the computer ask for
a word.
2. The ? sign is the
way the computer
asks for a word.
3. The word given
then goes into
memory address A$.

SPECIAL FEATURES

Mort Puce

My advice

My advice is to look at new commands carefully. When you think you understand the idea, experiment and try things out. You will learn what looks right. Of course, when you work like this you may create a mess. Don't be put off: try again. Remember your successes and forget about your failures.

Try out all the ideas you can think of. Explore lines, angles, shapes, colours and even music. You can draw almost anything on the screen and colour it in different ways and then to celebrate your masterpiece compose a tune or even a complete symphony.

When you hit on a good idea make sure you write some notes about it, so that you will be able to use the idea again.

Mort Puce

Changing the screen

The way in which characters are written out on the screen depends on the mode in which the computer is operating. When switched on the BBC microcomputer is in mode 7. In mode 7 there are 40 characters to the screen line and 25 lines on the screen. However, the computer will operate in other modes.

To change the mode, type MODE followed by the number of the mode required. For example, MODE 5 followed by [RETURN] puts the computer into MODE 5. Changing modes will remove anything that is already on the screen.

You try

Type MODE 5 then press [RETURN] . Type PRINT (notice the change). Try out MODE 4 and MODE 6 in the same way.

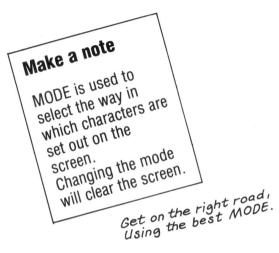

Make a note

MODE is used to select the way in which characters are set out on the screen.
Changing the mode will clear the screen.

Get on the right road,
Using the best MODE.

Drawing on the screen

The DRAW statement is used to draw lines and shapes. DRAW operates in MODE 4 and MODE 5, but usually MODE 4 gives better results. To make the computer draw, the DRAW statement must be followed by two numbers separated by a comma.
For example,
DRAW 4ØØ,6ØØ
DRAW 75Ø,22Ø

For lines to draw,
Set up MODE 4.

The first number can be any whole number from Ø to 1279. The second can be any whole number from Ø to 1Ø23.

The DRAW statement operates in a similar way to drawing on a piece of paper, without lifting the pencil. The first number after DRAW gives the distance across, and the second number gives the distance up the screen at which the line finishes.

You try

Type MODE 4 then press [RETURN]. Type DRAW 1279,1023 then press [RETURN].

Make a start,
On computer art.

This is what will appear on the screen:

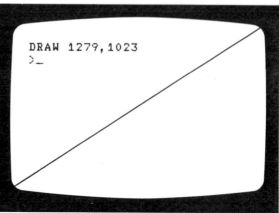

```
DRAW 1279,1023
>_
```

You try

Type MODE 4 then press [RETURN].
Type DRAW 500,0 then press [RETURN].
Type DRAW 0,500 then press [RETURN].
Type DRAW 0,0 then press [RETURN].

This is what will appear on the screen:

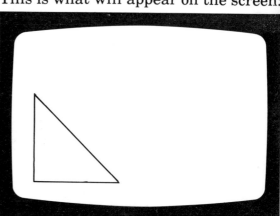

You try

Type MODE 4 then press [RETURN].
Type DRAW 100,0 then press [RETURN].
Type DRAW 100,100 then press [RETURN].
Type DRAW 0,100 then press [RETURN].
Type DRAW 0,0 then press [RETURN].

This is what will appear on the screen:

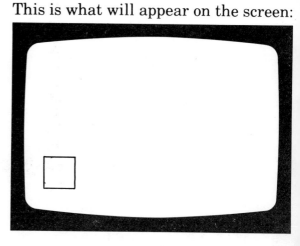

Moving on the screen

The MOVE statement is used to move on the screen without drawing a line. When using the DRAW statement you will find from time to time that you need to MOVE to another point on the screen without actually drawing a line. This can be done using MOVE. Just as DRAW was like drawing on a piece of paper without lifting the pencil, MOVE allows you to take the pencil off the paper and start to DRAW again at another point.

This is what will appear on the screen:

You try

Type MODE 4 then press RETURN .
Type MOVE Ø,512 then press RETURN .
Type DRAW 1279,Ø then press RETURN .

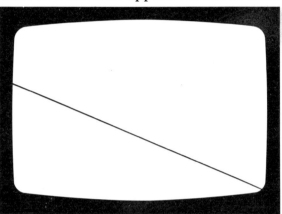

This is what will appear on the screen:

You try

Type MODE 4 then press RETURN .
Type DRAW 1279,512 then press RETURN .
Type MOVE 1279,Ø then press RETURN .
Type DRAW Ø,512 then press RETURN .

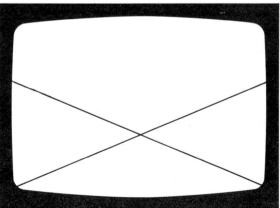

41

To help you plan your drawings, a grid showing distances across and up the screen is given below.

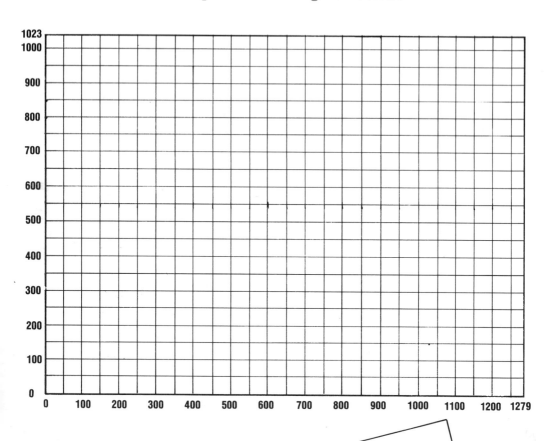

You try

Use the DRAW and the MOVE statements together to draw a house or a road sign.

If you've liked this a lot,
Then refer to term PLOT.

Make a note

The MOVE and DRAW statements must be followed by two numbers.
First number Ø to 1279
Second number Ø to 1Ø23
These two numbers must be separated by a comma.

BBC User Guide 319

The first number gives the distance across the screen and the second number the distance up the screen of your final position.

If you are really interested in exploring other ideas like DRAW and MOVE then refer to PLOT in the **BBC User Guide**.

Changing colours

The COLOUR statement is used to change the colours on the screen. COLOUR operates in MODE 5. The main colours available are black, red, white and yellow.
These colours only operate if you have a colour monitor or a colour TV. If you are using a black and white monitor or a black and white TV, then the red and yellow will appear as different shades of grey.
Usually the computer displays white characters on a black background. The colour of the characters and the background can be set using the COLOUR statement.

You try

The 'You try' exercise gives red characters on a white background. Try telling the computer to PRINT your name so that you can see the effect.

Type MODE 5 then press RETURN .
Type COLOUR 1 then press RETURN .
Type COLOUR 131 then press RETURN .

To bring colours alive!
Set up MODE 5.

You try

The 'You try' exercise gives yellow characters on a red background.

Type MODE 5 then press RETURN .
Type COLOUR 2 then press RETURN .
Type COLOUR 129 then press RETURN .

The COLOUR of the characters can be set by using
COLOUR Ø   (black)
COLOUR 1   (red)
COLOUR 2   (yellow)
COLOUR 3   (white)

43

The COLOUR of the background can be set by using
COLOUR 128 (black)
COLOUR 129 (red)
COLOUR 13Ø (yellow)
COLOUR 131 (white)

You try

Use MODE 5 and the COLOUR statements to set up your own colours.

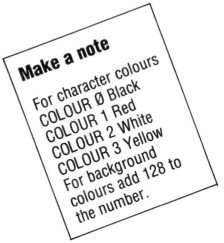

Make a note

For character colours
COLOUR Ø Black
COLOUR 1 Red
COLOUR 2 White
COLOUR 3 Yellow
For background colours add 128 to the number.

WARNING! If your character colour and background colour are the same, then anything you type will not appear on the screen.

Making music

BBC User Guide 347

The SOUND statement is used to play musical notes. SOUND operates equally well in all MODES, so there is no need to select any particular MODE. The SOUND statement is followed by four numbers which are separated by commas. For example,

SOUND 1,–15,1Ø,25Ø
SOUND 2,–5,25Ø,2Ø

The first number selects the instrument. All instruments sound alike. By using different instruments it is possible to play two notes at the same time. The numbers used are 1, 2 and 3.

The second number selects how loud the sound is (called the volume). The numbers used are Ø to –15, where –15 is the loudest.

The third number selects how high or low the sound is (called the pitch). The numbers used are Ø to 255, where 255 gives the highest note.

The fourth number selects the length of time the sound is played. The numbers used are Ø to 254 where 254 gives the longest note.

It is the number at four,
Which plays the note more.

You try

Type SOUND 1,–15,1Ø,25Ø then press RETURN .

You try

Type SOUND 1,–5,25Ø,2Ø then press RETURN .

You try

Use the SOUND statement to play some of your own notes.

The 'You try' exercise plays a loud, low, long note.

The 'You try' exercise plays a soft, high, short note.

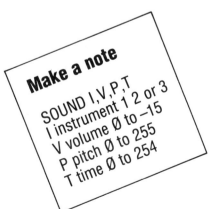

You can get the computer to play notes one after the other by using the : sign. For example,

SOUND 1,–15,1Ø,25Ø:SOUND 1,–5,25Ø,2Ø.

By using different instruments the computer can play two notes at once. For example:
SOUND 1,–15,1Ø, 25Ø:SOUND 2,–5,25Ø,2Ø.

You try

Use the SOUND statement and the : sign to play some notes one after the other or at the same time and compose a short tune.

Make a note

SOUND I,V,P,T
I instrument 1 2 or 3
V volume Ø to –15
P pitch Ø to 255
T time Ø to 254

WRITING PROGRAMS

Prof. O. Crumpet

My advice

You want ideas that work. You will probably need to spend some time thinking about them. If your idea does not work as you thought it would, then try to find out why. It may be that one very small alteration will make it work exactly as you intended.

However, it could be that your idea will never work, no matter how you alter it, so be prepared at times to start all over again. Sorting out ideas is not easy, but it is easier if you have some plan to work to.

Often an idea does not work quite as you wanted, but it could be used in another way. Make a note of it so that you can use it later. You must, of course, keep a very careful record of all your really good ideas.

Oliven Crumpet

The computer can do many things. Here are just a few. Try them for yourself. **BBC User Guide 28**

CLS (followed by RETURN) gives a blank screen.

PRINT (followed by RETURN) gives a blank line.

PRINT "COMPUTER" (followed by RETURN) gives the print out of COMPUTER.

PRINT "PROGRAMMER" (followed by RETURN) gives the print out of PROGRAMMER.

The computer can be given many other things to do, but instead of giving them to the computer one at a time, they can be given together. When the computer is given a list of things to do in order it is called a computer program. The lines begin with line numbers to tell the computer the order in which they should be carried out. Examples of line numbers are: 1Ø 2Ø 3Ø 4Ø 5Ø 6Ø etc.

The computer looks at the list and works through it 1Ø, 2Ø, 3Ø, 4Ø, 5Ø, 6Ø in order until it reaches the end. Some programs have just a few line numbers, other programs may have hundreds or even thousands. An example of a program is

```
1Ø CLS
2Ø PRINT
3Ø PRINT "COMPUTER"
4Ø PRINT
5Ø PRINT "PROGRAMMER"
6Ø PRINT
```

You are making a start,
At the programming art.

This is what will appear on the screen:

You try

Type the program above, line by line. After you have written a complete line press RETURN to go to the start of the next line.

```
>10 CLS
>20 PRINT
>30 PRINT "COMPUTER"
>40 PRINT
>50 PRINT "PROGRAMMER"
>60 PRINT
>_
```

You try

Now type the word
RUN and press
RETURN .

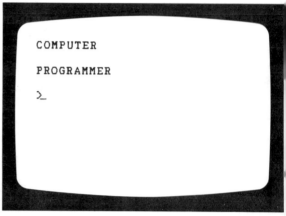

```
COMPUTER

PROGRAMMER

>_
```

If you have made any mistakes you can correct them by
re-typing the line in which they occur. Suppose your screen
showed

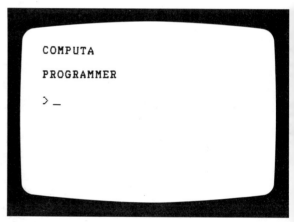

```
COMPUTA

PROGRAMMER

> _
```

The mistake is in line number 3Ø, so by re-typing the line
number 3Ø this mistake can be corrected.
3Ø PRINT "COMPUTER"
(followed by RETURN).
This will correct the line in the program and give you the
correct display.
You may also alter lines in the program in the same way.
Type in the following.
3Ø PRINT "A COMPUTER"
(followed by RETURN).
This will alter the line in the program.
While you are writing programs it is quite useful to be able
to look back at the program you have written. To do this
type the word LIST (followed by RETURN).

To find things missed, Just type LIST.

This is what will appear on the screen:

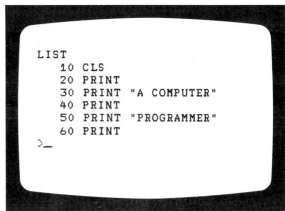

```
LIST
    10  CLS
    20  PRINT
    30  PRINT  "A COMPUTER"
    40  PRINT
    50  PRINT  "PROGRAMMER"
    60  PRINT
>_
```

The program line numbers go up in tens so it is possible to add extra lines. For example, try typing
15 PRINT "I AM" (followed by RETURN).
This puts the line into the program as follows.
1Ø CLS
15 PRINT "I AM"
2Ø PRINT
3Ø PRINT "A COMPUTER"
4Ø PRINT
5Ø PRINT "PROGRAMMER"
6Ø PRINT
You can check that this has been done by typing LIST followed by RETURN . Type RUN followed by RETURN .

Make a note

1. Number each line 1Ø, 2Ø, 3Ø etc.
2. Press RETURN when the line is complete.
3. Type RUN and press RETURN when the program is complete.
4. Correct mistakes by re-typing the line.
5. Type LIST and press RETURN to look at the program.

This is what will appear on the screen:

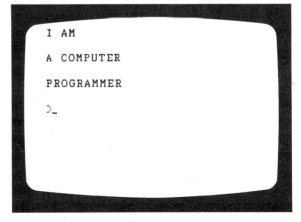

```
I AM

A COMPUTER

PROGRAMMER

>_
```

49

Writing programs

In order to write your own programs you need to find out just what the computer can do. The exercises which follow should help you.

Before you start the next section you need to have understood the last section. If you are at all unsure about anything, work through it again.

Type in these programs just as the earlier program was typed in, that is one line at a time followed by RETURN to get to the start of the next line. Check your program when it has all been typed in and correct any mistakes by re-writing the faulty line. When you are sure that the program is complete and correct type RUN and press RETURN and see what happens.

So that the computer does not get one program confused with the next, type NEW and press RETURN before typing in a new program. The computer then forgets the old program.

When you have copied and run the programs in each section then try the exercises. If you come up with any ideas for similar programs then try them out and see how they work.

At the end of this chapter there are five projects which are ideas for longer and more interesting programs. For most of the projects, you are helped with writing the basic program, and then you are given some ideas to improve it.

To see what is done,
Just type RUN.

Programs using PRINT

PRINT is used to print out lists, information, diagrams and instructions.

You try

Type NEW then press [RETURN] .
Type in the following program.
You may need to press [CAPS LOCK]
to be able to type small
letters. It is important to type all
commands in capitals or the
computer will not understand you.
10 CLS
20 PRINT "Pru Comet"
30 PRINT "P.C. Truemo"
40 PRINT "Mort Puce"
50 PRINT "O. Crumpet"
60 PRINT "O.C. Termup"
Type RUN then press [RETURN] .

This is what will appear on the screen:

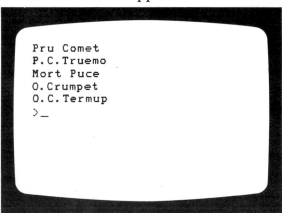

When writing a program, you
Must remember to start with NEW.

You try

Type NEW then press [RETURN] .
Type in the following program.
10 CLS
20 PRINT " . . . . "
30 PRINT " . 0   0   . "
40 PRINT " .   V   . "
50 PRINT " .   ===   . "
60 PRINT " . . . . "
Type RUN then press [RETURN] .

This is what will appear on the screen:

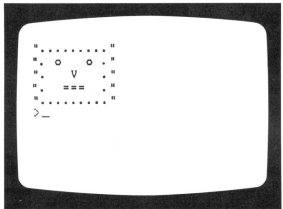

You try

Make up your own programs using
PRINT to do the following:

1. Write out a shopping list.
2. Design a motor-way sign.
3. Draw a space shuttle.

51

Programs using TAB

TAB is used to set out information or diagrams.

You try

Type NEW then press [RETURN] .
Type in the following program.
10 CLS
20 PRINT TAB(10) "Prof. O.
Crumpet"
30 PRINT TAB(13) "14 Mep
Court,"
40 PRINT TAB(16) "Portcume."
Type RUN then press [RETURN] .

This is what will appear on the screen

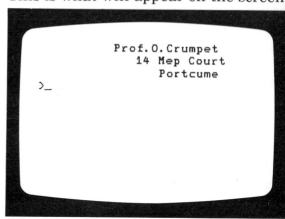

You try

Type NEW then press [RETURN] .
Type in the following program.
10 CLS
20 PRINT TAB(19) "*"
30 PRINT TAB(18) "***"
40 PRINT TAB(17) "*****"
50 PRINT TAB(16) "*******"
60 PRINT TAB(15) "*********"
Type RUN then press [RETURN] .

This is what will appear on the screen:

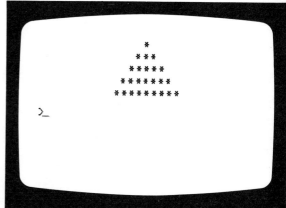

You try

Make up your own programs using
TAB to do the following.
1. Draw a staircase
2. Set out your address.
3. Draw a sloping line.

Programs using LET

LET is used to put a number into an address.

This is what will appear on the screen:

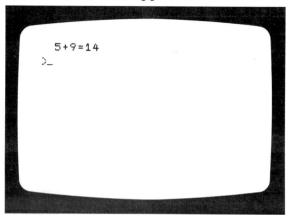

```
5+9=14
>_
```

ou try

pe NEW then press RETURN .
pe in the following program.
∅ CLS
∅ LET A=5
∅ LET B=9
∅ LET sum=A+B
∅ PRINT A;"+";B;"=";sum
pe RUN then press RETURN .

This is what will appear on the screen:

```
3X8=24
>_
```

ou try

pe NEW then press RETURN .
pe in the following program.
∅ CLS
∅ LET E=3
∅ LET F=8
∅ LET product=E*F
∅ PRINT E;"x";F;"=";product
pe RUN then press RETURN.

ou try

ake up your own programs using
T to do the following.
Add two other numbers.
Multiply two other numbers.
Subtract or divide numbers.

LET is also used to put words in addresses.

This is what will appear on the scree

You try

Type NEW then press RETURN .
Type in the following program.
10 CLS
20 LET A$="Martin"
30 LET B$="James"
40 LET C$="Thomas"
50 PRINT A$" "B$" "C$
60 PRINT C$" "B$" "A$
Type RUN then press RETURN .

```
Martin James Thomas
Thomas James Martin
> _
```

This is what will appear on the scree

You try

Type NEW then press RETURN .
Type in the following program.
10 CLS
20 LET A$="Can"
30 LET B$="You"
40 LET C$="Go"
50 PRINT A$" "B$" "C$
60 PRINT B$" "A$" "C$
Type RUN then press RETURN .

```
Can You Go
You Can Go
>
```

You try

Make up your own programs using LET to do the following.
1. Make A$="in", B$="on", C$="set", D$="side", E$="to", F$="up", G$="wards". By putting these words together, see how many longer words you can print.
2. Make sentences from words.
3. Select items from a menu.

Programs using INPUT

INPUT is used to put numbers into programs.

This is what will appear on the screen:

ou try

ype NEW then press [RETURN] .
ype in the following program.
Ø CLS
Ø INPUT A
Ø INPUT B
Ø LET difference=A−B
Ø PRINT A;"−";B;"=";difference
ype RUN then press [RETURN] .

ou try

ype in a number,
or example 9, then
ress [RETURN] .
ype in a number,
or example 7, then
ress [RETURN] .

This is what will appear on the screen:

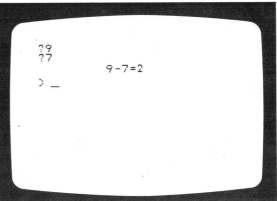

```
?9
?7
        9−7=2
>_
```

ou try

low put your own numbers into
he program.

You try

Type NEW then press ⎡RETURN⎤ .
Type in the following program.
10 CLS
20 INPUT N
30 INPUT D
40 LET quotient=N/D
50 PRINT N;"/";D;"=";quotient
Type RUN then press ⎡RETURN⎤ .

This is what will appear on the screen

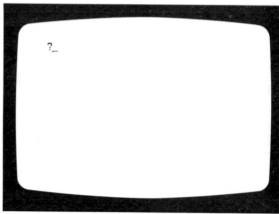

You try

Type in a number, for example 8,
then press ⎡RETURN⎤ .
Type in a number, for example 4,
then press ⎡RETURN⎤ .

This is what will appear on the screen

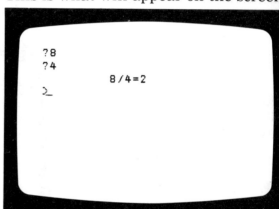

You try

Type RUN then press ⎡RETURN⎤ .
Now put your own numbers into
the program.

You try

Make up your own programs using
INPUT to do the following.
1. Add two numbers together.
2. Multiply two numbers.
3. Ask for the amount of pocket
money you receive in a week and
multiply this by 52 to give the
amount you receive in a year.

INPUT is also used to put words into programs.

This is what will appear on the screen:

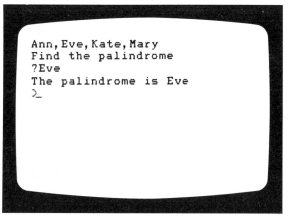

```
Ann,Eve,Kate,Mary
Find the palindrome
?_
```

ou try

ype NEW then press ⌊RETURN⌋ .
ype in the following program.
Ø CLS
Ø PRINT "Ann,Eve,Kate,Mary"
Ø PRINT "Find the palindrome."
Ø INPUT answer$.
Ø PRINT "The palindrome is
ve."
ype RUN then press ⌊RETURN⌋ .

This is what will appear on the screen:

```
Ann,Eve,Kate,Mary
Find the palindrome
?Eve
The palindrome is Eve
>_
```

ou try

ype in the
alindrome Eve then
ress ⌊RETURN⌋ .

A palindrome is a word which is spelt the same way
ackwards as forwards.)

You try

Type NEW then press [RETURN] .
Type in the following program.
10 CLS
20 PRINT "Give me a word to fit this sentence."
30 PRINT "Today the weather is "
40 INPUT answer$.
50 PRINT "Today the weather is ";answer

When a line is too long to fit on the screen just keep typing normally and the computer will sort it out. Do not press [RETURN] until you have reached the end of the instruction.
Type RUN then press [RETURN] .

This is what will appear on the screen

You try

Type in sunny (or another word to describe the weather) then press [RETURN] .

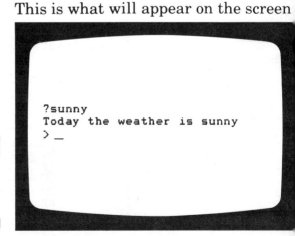

You try

Make up your own programs using INPUT to do the following.
1. Find a missing word.
2. Answer a simple question.
3. Make the computer have a conversation with you.

Programs using LEFT$, MID$ and RIGHT$

The word functions LEFT$, MID$ and RIGHT$ can be used to pick out parts of words.

This is what will appear on the screen:

You try

Type NEW then press [RETURN] .
Type in the following program.
10 CLS
20 LET word$="composer"
30 PRINT LEFT$(word$,7)
40 PRINT RIGHT$(word$,5)
50 PRINT MID$(word$,4,4)
Type RUN then press [RETURN] .
Use LEFT$, MID$ and RIGHT$ to
PRINT as many words as you can
if word$="another".

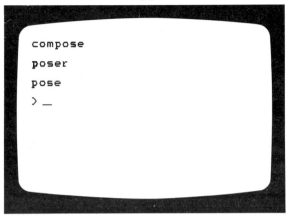

Programs using RND (random numbers)

BBC User Guide 342

RND is used to choose random numbers.

This is what may appear on the screen:

You try

Type NEW then press [RETURN] .
Type in the following program.
10 CLS
20 LET first=RND(6)
30 LET second=RND(6)
40 PRINT "FIRST DICE";first
50 PRINT "SECOND DICE";second
Type RUN then press [RETURN] .

The instruction "LET first=RND(6)" chooses one of the numbers 1, 2, 3, 4, 5, 6 at random and puts the chosen number into the address "first".

59

The computer chooses random numbers and it is unlikely that it will choose the numbers shown on the previous page, but it will choose two numbers from one to six. Try running the program several times and different numbers will probably be chosen.

This is what may appear on the screen

You try

Type NEW then press RETURN .
10 CLS
20 LET Leeds=RND(3)
30 LET Arsenal=RND(3)
40 PRINT "LEEDS";Leeds
50 PRINT "ARSENAL";Arsenal
Type RUN then press RETURN .

```
LEEDS3
ARSENAL1
> _
```

Again the computer will choose numbers at random and it is unlikely that the above score will be shown.

You try

Make up your own program using RND to do the following.
1. Choose a winning raffle ticket from 1000 tickets.
2. Select numbers for a game of Bingo (numbers 1 to 90).
3. Make up sums and print the correct answer when you have had a go.

Programs using FOR/NEXT/STEP

FOR/NEXT/STEP is used to repeat the same lines in turn for a set of numbers.

This is what will appear on the screen:

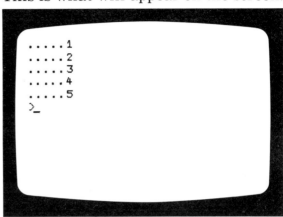

ou try

pe NEW then press [RETURN] .
pe in the following program.
⅃ CLS
⅃ FOR count=1 TO 5 STEP 1
⅃ PRINT " . . . . . ";count
⅃ NEXT count
pe RUN then press [RETURN] .

For each value of count between 1 and 5, the row of dots and value of count was printed.

This is what will appear on the screen:

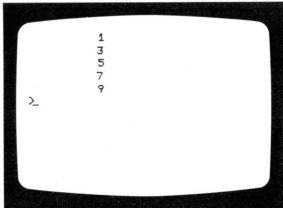

ou try

pe NEW then press [RETURN] .
pe in the following program.
Ø CLS
Ø FOR N=1 TO 9 STEP 2
Ø PRINT N
Ø NEXT N
pe RUN then press [RETURN] .

ou try

ake up your own programs using
⅃R/NEXT/STEP to do the
llowing.
. Print out the numbers 1 to 20.
. Print out your name and
ddress three times.
. Print out the three times table.

If you do not tell the computer the size of the step it assumes "STEP 1", so we could have left this out in the first example.

61

Programs using DATA/READ

DATA/READ is used to put data (information) into the computer and read (recall) it when it is needed.

This is what will appear on the screen

```
here    is     a     clue
a       clue   is    here
> _
```

You try

Type NEW then press [RETURN] .
Type in the following program.
10 CLS
20 DATA is,clue,a,here
30 READ W$,X$,Y$,Z$
40 PRINT Z$,W$,Y$,X$
50 PRINT Y$,X$,W$,Z$
Type RUN then press [RETURN] .

This is what will appear on the screen

```
pupil 1 has an average mark of 68
pupil 2 has an average mark of 81
pupil 3 has an average mark of 71
pupil 4 has an average mark of 80
pupil 5 has an average mark of 79
> _
```

You try

Type in the following program which, for each of five pupils, reads in their maths mark and English mark and works out the average.
10 CLS
20 DATA 75,61,83,79,
64,78,93,67,86,72
30 FOR pupil=1 TO 5
40 READ maths, English
50 LET
average=(maths+English)/2
60 PRINT ''pupil '';pupil;'' has an average mark of''; average
70 NEXT pupil
Type RUN then press [RETURN] .

You try

Make up your own programs using READ/DATA to do the following:

1. Rearrange a list of items.
2. Make a list of months giving the number of days in each month.

Programs using REPEAT/UNTIL

REPEAT/UNTIL is used to repeat lines of the program until a particular condition is satisfied.

This is what will appear on the screen:

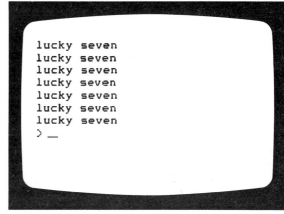

You try

Type NEW then press RETURN .
Type in the following program.

```
1Ø CLS
2Ø LET count=Ø
3Ø REPEAT PRINT "lucky seven"
4Ø LET count=count+1
5Ø UNTIL count=7
```

Type RUN then press RETURN .

The particular condition to be satisfied in the 'You try' above is that "count=7". The program will repeat lines 2Ø and 3Ø until count=7.

The next 'You try' uses two new ideas. The first is a method of putting two words together, which we do by putting '+' between them. For example, if X$="Prof.", then X$+"Crumpet" gives "Prof. Crumpet".

Secondly, to find out the number of symbols in X$ we use LEN(X$). If X$="Prof." as before, then LEN(X$)=5. LEN tells us how many spaces a word takes up on the screen.

This is what will appear on the screen:

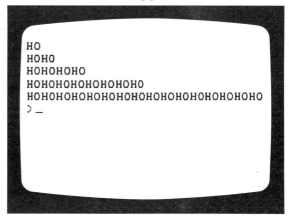

You try

Type NEW then press RETURN .

```
1Ø CLS
2Ø LET B$="HO"
3Ø REPEAT
4Ø PRINT B$
5Ø LET B$=B$+B$
6Ø UNTIL LEN(B$)>4Ø
```

Type RUN then press RETURN .

Make up your own programs using REPEAT/UNTIL to do the following.
1. Print out the numbers 1 to 2Ø.

2. Print the question "What is 10×4" and input the answer until the correct answer is given.

Programs using IF/THEN/ELSE BBC User Guide 272

IF/THEN/ELSE is used to introduce alternatives.

This is what will appear on the screen:

```
Type WORD
?
```

You try

Type NEW then press RETURN .
Type in the following program.
10 CLS
20 PRINT ''Type WORD''
30 INPUT word$
40 IF word$=''WORD'' THEN
PRINT ''correct'' ELSE PRINT
''wrong''
Type RUN then press RETURN .

This is what will appear on the screen:

You try

Type WORD then press RETURN .

```
Type WORD
?WORD
correct
>_
```

Notice that you must type
'WORD' in capitals for this to
work. Run the program again.

This is what will appear on the screen:

You try

Type WIRD then press RETURN .

```
?WIRD
wrong
>_
```

64

You try

Type NEW then press [RETURN] .
Type in the following program.
10 CLS
20 PRINT "6X4="
30 INPUT answer
40 IF answer = 24 THEN PRINT
"correct" ELSE PRINT "wrong"
Type RUN then press [RETURN] .

This is what will appear on the screen:

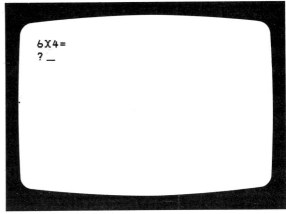

```
6X4=
? _
```

You try

Type 24 then press [RETURN] .

This is what will appear on the screen:

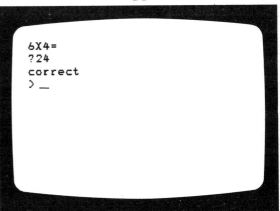

```
6X4=
?24
correct
> _
```

Run the program again.

You try

Type 36 then press [RETURN] .

This is what will appear on the screen:

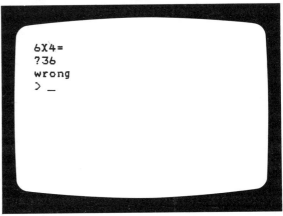

```
6X4=
?36
wrong
> _
```

You try

Make up your own programs using
IF/THEN/ELSE to do the following.
1. Check an answer to a simple
question.
2. Make the computer ask if you
are well and give a suitable reply to
your answer.

Programs using GOTO

GOTO is used to jump to a different line in the program.

You try

Type NEW then press [RETURN] .
Type in the following program.
10 CLS
20 PRINT "Type in a number."
30 INPUT number
40 IF number <100 THEN GOTO 70
50 PRINT number "is more than 99"
60 END
70 PRINT number "is less than 100"
Type RUN then press [RETURN] .

This is what will appear on the screen

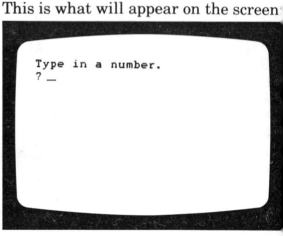

```
Type in a number.
? _
```

This is what will appear on the screen:

You try

Type in a number, for example 71,
then press [RETURN] .

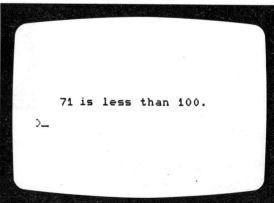

```
        71 is less than 100.
     >_
```

You try

Type NEW then press [RETURN] .
Type in the following program.
10 CLS
20 PRINT "7×7= "
30 INPUT answer
40 IF answer=49 THEN GOTO 70
50 PRINT "wrong"
60 GOTO 20
70 PRINT "correct"
Type RUN then press [RETURN] .

This is what will appear on the screen:

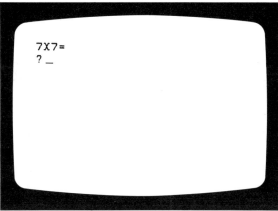

```
7X7=
? _
```

You try

Type in your answer then press
[RETURN] .

This is what will appear on the screen:

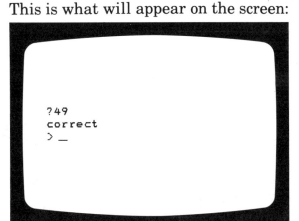

```
?49
correct
> _
```

You try

Make up your own programs using
GOTO to do the following.
1. Print Yes or No in answer to a
question.
2. Print a word in small or in
capital letters.
3. Input the cost of five items of
shopping and print the total cost.
You will need to make the
computer keep count of the
number of items input so far.

Programs using AND

AND is used to check two conditions.

This is what will appear on the screen:

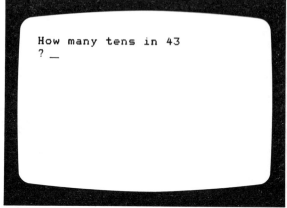

```
How many tens in 43
? _
```

You try

Type NEW then press [RETURN] .
Type in the following program.
10 CLS
20 REPEAT PRINT "How many
tens in 43"
30 INPUT tens
40 PRINT "How many units in 43"
50 INPUT units
60 UNTIL tens=4 AND units=3
70 PRINT "Both correct"
Type RUN then press [RETURN] .

This is what will appear on the screen:

```
How many tens in 43
?4
How many units in 43
?3
Both correct
>
```

You try

Type 4 then press [RETURN] .
Type 3 then press [RETURN] .

You try

Run the program again.
Type in one or two incorrect
answers and notice what happens.

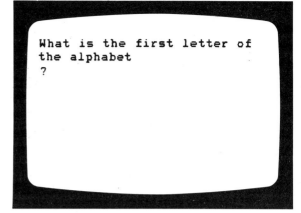

You try

Type NEW then press [RETURN] .
Type in the following program.
10 CLS
20 PRINT "What is the first letter
of the alphabet"
30 INPUT A$
40 PRINT "What is the last letter
of the alphabet"
50 INPUT Z$
60 IF A$="A" AND Z$="Z"
THEN PRINT "both correct" ELSE
GOTO 20
Type RUN then press [RETURN] .

This is what will appear on the screen:

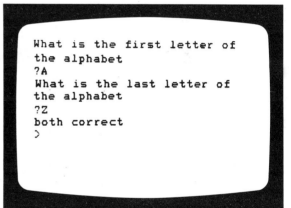

You try

Type A then press [RETURN] .
Type Z then press [RETURN] .

You try

Run the program again.
Type in one or two incorrect letters
and notice what happens.

You try

Make up your own programs using AND to
do the following:
1. To check for two possible answers to a
question.
2. To select two words from a list of words.
3. To select two numbers from a list of
numbers.

Programs using OR

OR is used to check for one of two conditions.

You try

Type NEW then press [RETURN] .
Type in the following program.
10 CLS
20 PRINT "Which letter makes an"
30 PRINT "animal MO.SE"
40 INPUT letter$
50 IF letter$="U" OR
letter$="O" THEN PRINT
"correct" ELSE GOTO 20
Type RUN then press [RETURN] .

This is what will appear on the screen

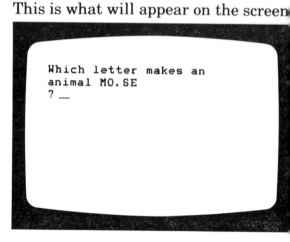

```
Which letter makes an
animal MO.SE
? _
```

You try

Type O then press [RETURN] .

Run the program again.

This is what will appear on the screen:

```
? O
correct
> _
```

You try

Type U then press [RETURN] .

You try

Type in incorrect answers and
notice what happens.

This is what will appear on the screen:

```
?U
correct
> _
```

This is what will appear on the screen:

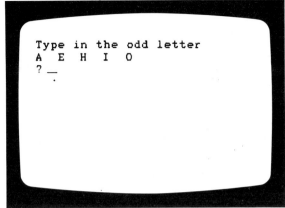

```
Type in the odd letter
A   E   H   I   O
? _
```

You try

Type NEW then press [RETURN] .
Type in the following program.
```
10 CLS
20 REPEAT PRINT "Type in the
odd letter"
30 PRINT "A E H I O"
40 INPUT letter$
50 UNTIL letter$="E" OR
letter$="H"
60 PRINT "correct"
```
Type RUN then press [RETURN] .

This is what will appear on the screen:

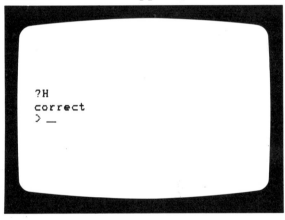

```
?H
correct
> _
```

You try

Type H then press [RETURN] .

You try

Run the program again and try typing in other letters.

Make up your own programs using OR to do the following.
1. Check for one of two possible answers to a question.
2. Check an answer which may be written in either small or capital letters.
3. Check a numerical answer which may be one of two numbers.

71

Project 1 – Knock, knock

The aim of this program is to make the computer tell knock, knock jokes. The main structure is a large REPEAT ... UNTIL loop, but first it is necessary to set up some starting values and give some data. The main steps are given below.

1. LET count=Ø (We are going to count the number of jokes so that we know when we have reached the end. This is to start the count. We shall increase the count by one each time a joke is told.)
LET jokes=6 (This gives the number of jokes the computer can tell.)
DATA Ivor, sore hand from knocking on your door, Howard, I know, Mr, last bus home, Amos, quito, Lettuce, in and you'll find out, Ken, I come in

2. Now we can set up the REPEAT ... UNTIL loop. Start with the instruction REPEAT, then inside the loop the computer should be made to
    (a) ask if you want to hear a knock, knock joke
    (b) INPUT the answer
    (c) if the answer is 'no' then END
    (d) otherwise READ name$, lastline$
    (e) PRINT Knock, knock
                Who's there?
                name$
                name$ who?
                name$; lastline$
      (This will take several PRINT statements.)
    (f) LET count=count+1 (increasing count by one).
The loop continues UNTIL count=jokes.

Improvements and variations

A. Add some more jokes.

B. Make the telling of the jokes into a conversation with the computer. Then the computer will PRINT 'Knock, knock', you will INPUT 'Who's there', etc.

C. Make the program END if the answer to 'Do you want to hear another joke?' is 'no' OR 'NO'.

D. Make the computer PRINT a message when it has run out of jokes to tell.

E. Include a pause between telling one joke and asking if you wish to hear another. This can be done by inserting the line FOR n=1 TO 5ØØØ:NEXT n
This makes the computer go round and round a loop which does nothing. Using a number greater than 5ØØØ would make the pause longer.

Project 2 – Drawing

There is a great deal that you can do using DRAW and MOVE. Here are some ideas.

A. Try drawing a picture of a space rocket, a church, a TV set, a castle, a ship, or a telephone kiosk. It is easier if you draw the picture first on a copy of the grid on page 42.

B. Draw a small star (using the grid on page 42 to help you). Try adding the same number to all the distances across (the first number after DRAW and MOVE). See where the star is drawn now. Then try to draw the star further up the screen.
By using a FOR...NEXT loop and RND try drawing many stars on the screen at random positions (so that it is different each time you run the program). If you have a colour TV set or monitor you can try making the stars different colours.

C. Try using

FOR line=1 TO 1ØØØ STEP 5Ø: MOVE Ø,line: DRAW 1279,line: NEXT line

to draw equally spaced lines going across the screen. Work out a similar program to draw lines down the screen. Put them together and you have a grid. You can do something similar to draw a ladder.

D. You can make a solid square by trying

FOR line=4ØØ TO 5ØØ: MOVE 5ØØ,line:
DRAW 6ØØ,line: NEXT line

Try a similar program to draw a solid rectangle.

E. Try writing out your name in large letters using DRAW and MOVE.

Project 3 – Countdown

In this project you will program the computer to play a game with you. In this game you start with 20 counters. You and the computer take it in turns to remove 1, 2, 3 or 4 counters. The one to remove the last counters so that none are left is the winner. The program can be written as follows.

1. Make the computer explain the game using PRINT.

2. Set up the number of counters to be 2Ø.

3. Have your turn which consists of the following steps.
    (a) Make the computer ask for the number of counters you wish to remove and INPUT the answer.
    (b) Take away your answer from the number of counters to give the number of counters remaining and PRINT the result.
    (c) Check whether the number of counters is zero. If it is then make the computer tell you that you have won and END the game.

4. Make the computer have a turn by doing the following steps.
    (a) If the number of counters is less than five (<5), then the computer can choose to remove all the counters. Otherwise the computer chooses to remove a random number of counters between 1 and 4 (use RND(4)). (Use IF/THEN/ELSE for this part.)
    (b) Calculate the new number of counters and PRINT the result.
    (c) Check whether the number of counters is zero. If it is then the computer says that it has won and ENDS the game, otherwise it returns to your turn (step 3). Make sure that the name for the number of counters is the same as at the beginning of step 3.

Improvements and variations

A. The computer could ask whether you want the first turn, and if not have the first turn itself.

B. Instead of having the computer write down the number of counters, make it draw the counters (use PRINT and the letter O as a counter).

C. Make the screen clearer by using CLS, PRINT on its own for a blank line, and extra spaces.

D. It would be a good idea to make the computer check that you are not cheating by trying to remove too many counters or none at all.

E. You could vary the number of counters at the start and the number which may be picked up at each turn.

F. When you have played the game a few times and know how to beat the computer, try making the computer play more intelligently.

Project 4 – Music

The object of this program is to play the tune Brother Joseph (Frère Jacques). The English words, with notes above, are given below.

```
   G  A  B  G    G  A  B  G
Brother Joseph, Brother Joseph,
```

```
   B   C' D'    B   C'  D'
Wake up now! Wake up now!
```

```
D' E' D' C'  B  G   D' E' D' C'  B   G
Go and pull the bell rope. Go and pull the bell rope.
```

```
   G  D  G    G   D   G
Ding, dang, dong. Ding, dang, dong.
```

Each note can be given to the computer as a command of the form SOUND 1, –15,pitch,time. Pitch says how high or low the note is, and time gives its length. The numbers for the pitch are

D	E	F	G	A	B	C'	D'	E'
61	69	73	81	89	97	1Ø1	1Ø9	117

The time should be 5 for the short notes, 1Ø for the medium length notes, and 2Ø for the long notes. If you find it difficult to decide on the timing, put the time to be 1Ø for all the notes at first, and make changes after listening.

Some suggestions for writing out this program are given below. You may find that some of them are useful.

(a) LET v=−15 at the beginning of the program and then use SOUND 1,v,pitch,time. This has the advantage that there is less typing, and it is possible to change the volume easily by changing the value of v.

(b) LET t=5 at the beginning of the program and then let time be given as t, 2*t or 4*t as appropriate (rather than 5, 1Ø or 2Ø). Then the speed at which the tune is played can be changed easily, by changing the value of t. The numbers multiplying t give the number of beats that the note lasts.

(c) The function keys can be set up to play specific notes (see page 21). For example, try typing
*KEYØ SOUND 1,−15,81,1Ø ¦M
then press RETURN . Then press ⌊fø⌋ and hear what happens.

(d) You can also try using DATA/READ in a similar way to their use in the Knock, knock project. This is a better way to program and needs less typing. It also makes it easier to change the key in which the tune is played, that is to play the tune higher or lower. However, it does make improvement C more difficult.

Improvements and variations

A. The tune probably sounds rather strange since there is no gap between the notes. If two notes with the same pitch are played immediately after each other, they sound like one long note. This can be improved by using SOUND 1,Ø,Ø,1 to put a short pause after each phrase (that is after the 4th note, 8th note, 11th note, etc.). This is easiest to do using one of the function keys (see page 21).

B You could make the words come up on the screen as the tune is being played by using PRINT. This could also help to make it easier to see where in the tune you have reached when you LIST the program.

C. You could make the computer play the tune as a round. This means that two instruments play the same tune, but starting at different times. For example, with the tune in this project the second instrument can start when the first

one reaches the beginning of the line 'Wake up now!'.
Setting up a round is quite tricky. The second instrument
is played by using SOUND 2,−15,pitch,time. It can be
made to play at the same time as the first instrument by
putting two SOUND statements on one line, separated by a
colon.†
Here is some advice for coping with some of the difficulties.

- **(a)** When the first instrument has a long note, you may
  need to put two SOUND statements for the second
  instrument on that line.
- **(b)** When the first instrument has short notes, there
  may be lines where no note is needed for the second
  instrument.
- **(c)** At the beginning when just the first instrument is
  playing, you may need to make the second
  instrument play a silent note (by using
  SOUND 2,Ø,Ø,1Ø) for each note that the first
  instrument plays.
- **(d)** Make sure that any pauses for the first instrument
  are also included for the second.

†This method can be made to make two instruments play
in time together, but it needs to be used carefully. There is
a better method for making sure that two instruments play
together, but it is more complicated. (See the **BBC User
Guide** page 350.)

Project 5 – Lions and antelopes

The purpose of this program is to set up a situation like the
one faced by the warden of a game park in Africa. We shall
look at the lions and antelopes in the game park. The lions
kill the antelopes for food (about 2ØØ each in a year), and
the warden has to choose how many lions to kill to keep
the numbers under control.
The structure of the program is as follows.

1. Make the computer explain the situation for someone
new coming to the program, using PRINT.

2. Give starting values for the number of lions and the
number of antelopes. It is sensible to start with about 15
lions and 1ØØØØ antelopes.

3. Make the computer ask for the number of lions to be
killed this year and INPUT the reply. This number is
called the cull.

4. Work out the number of lions and antelopes for the following year using the equations below.

LET lions=INT(lions−cull
+lions*(antelopes−4ØØ*lions)/1ØØØØ)

LET antelopes=INT(antelopes−2ØØ*lions
+antelopes*(2ØØØØ−antelopes)/3ØØØØ)

INT makes sure that the answer is a whole number. The equation for the lions says that the new number of lions is the number from the previous year, minus the number killed, plus a number of births and deaths depending on the number of lions available to breed and the number of antelopes available as food. The equation for the antelopes is the number from the previous year, minus the number killed by lions, plus the number of births and deaths. Make the computer PRINT the new number of lions and antelopes.

5. Make the computer ask if you want another go, and if so then go to step 3.

Improvements and variations

A. Alter the number of lions and antelopes at the start either by using INPUT so that the user chooses them, or by using RND so that the computer chooses them.

B. Make the computer keep a count of the year and PRINT the year number each time round. The computer could then ask if you wish to continue after every ten years, instead of every year.

C. Include a check that the number of lions and the number of antelopes do not become negative.

D. Include messages of congratulations if the number of lions and antelopes become large and scold the user if they become small.

E. Make the writing on the screen clearer by using CLS (to clear the screen), PRINT on its own (to give a blank line), and put in extra spaces between words so that no words are split between lines.

F. If you feel ambitious you could try drawing a picture of the park, and using symbols for lions and antelopes (say one symbol to represent a lion and another to represent 1ØØ antelopes).

Other ideas for computer programs

1. A game of chance which uses random (RND) numbers
2. A spelling test
3. A list of questions on a particular subject
4. A musical scale
5. A questionnaire
6. A coloured diagram
7. A science experiment
8. A clock
9. A cash register
10. An anagram finder
11. A language translater
12. A passage in which missing words have to be filled in
13. A pattern designer
14. A list of names and addresses
15. A plan or scale drawing
16. A word game
17. An alphabetical sorter
18. A number game with questions and answers
19. A foreign money exchange
20. A cartoon
21. A maze
22. A rocket launcher
23. A TV advert
24. A guessing game
25. A tune

You may need to look back at some of the programs in the book or ones which you have written yourself.
It may also be helpful to check certain things in the reference sections from time to time.

FINDING OUT

Always check
the terms you use.

Miss O.C. Termup

My advice

Always check the terms you use just as you would check the
meaning of unusual words with a dictionary. Most of the
terms are fairly easy to understand, but there are a lot of
them. If you are unsure then check the meaning and use.
All the terms you are likely to need are contained in the six
parts of the reference section. So first find out which section
the term is in and then look it up in that section.
The sections are

> Commands
> Statements
> Number functions
> Word functions
> Operators
> Geometric functions

It would be very useful if you made your own reference book
to contain all the terms you come across. You need not put
them in separate sections, but it will make things much
easier if they are in alphabetical order.

Olive C. Termup

Reference sections

The terms which you have used in the book will all be found in the reference sections, but you will also find some new terms. These are included because they may be useful when you are writing your own programs.

If you are writing a program which examines words, then you might find some of the word function terms very useful. In a mathematics program some of the geometric function terms will be very useful.

The reference sections only give a brief outline of the meaning and use of the terms and if you wish to find out more about them you will have to look them up in other books. The list below is given for this purpose.

The BBC Microcomputer User Guide
Author John Coll
BBC ISBN 0 563 16558 8

Basic Programming on the BBC Microcomputer
Authors Neil and Pat Cryer
Prentice Hall International ISBN 0 13 066407 3

Let Your BBC Micro Teach You to Program
Author Tim Hartnell
Interface Publications ISBN 0 907563 14 7

Games BBC Computers Play
Authors Tim Hartnell, S.M. Gee and Mike James
Interface Publications/Addison-Wesley
Publishing Company ISBN 0 201 14640 1

30+ Programs for the BBC Microcomputer
Author Chris Evans
CJE Microcomputers ISBN 0 946190 00 3

There are also a number of computer magazines which can be very helpful. Quite regularly they list programs which you might find interesting and you may well be able to adapt these programs to your own needs. Some suitable magazines are

Personal Computer World
Personal Computing Today
Computer and Video Games

Your Computer
Acorn User
BBC Micro User

Here is a list of all the terms that the BBC computer understands. The ones in heavy type are those which are likely to be most useful to you. These are the ones described more fully in the following pages. Wait to use the other terms until you have learnt more about BASIC.

1. Commands	2. Statements	DRAW
		ELSE
AUTO	CALL	**END**
DELETE	CHAIN	**ENDPROC**
LIST	CLEAR	ENVELOPE
LISTO	CLG	**FN**
LOAD	**CLS**	**FOR**
NEW	**COLOUR**	GCOL
OLD	**DATA**	**GOSUB**
RENUMBER	**DEF**	**GOTO**
SAVE	**DIM**	HIMEM

IF
INPUT
LET
LOCAL
LOMEM
MODE
MOVE
NEXT
ON
OPT
PAGE
PLOT
PRINT
PROC
READ
REM
REPEAT
REPORT
RESTORE
RETURN
RUN
SOUND
STEP
STOP
THEN
TO
TOP
TRACE
UNTIL
USR
VDU

3. Number functions

ABS
ADVAL
COUNT
ERL
ERR
EVAL
FALSE
GET
INKEY
INT
MOD
PI
POINT
POS
RND
SGN
SPC
SQR
TAB
TIME
TRUE
VAL
VPOS
WIDTH

4. Word functions

ASC
CHR$
GET$
INKEY$
INSTR
LEFT$
LEN
MID$
RIGHT$
STR$
STRING$

5. Operators

AND
DIV
EOR
NOT
OR

6. Geometric functions

ACS
ASN
ATN
COS
DEG
EXP
LN
LOG
RAD
SIN
TAN

7. File statements

BGET#
BPUT#
CLOSE#
EOF#
EXT#
INPUT#
OPENIN
OPENOUT
PRINT#
PTR#

Commands

AUTO enters line numbers without first typing in the number of the line. It can be ended by pressing ESCAPE .
AUTO   gives 1Ø,2Ø,3Ø . . . . etc.
AUTO 12Ø   gives 12Ø,13Ø,14Ø . . etc.
AUTO 12Ø,4   gives 12Ø,124,128, . . . etc.
AUTO ,2 gives 1Ø,12,14,16 . . . . . . etc.
BBC User Guide 211

DELETE deletes lines from a program.
DELETE 2Ø,3Ø   deletes all lines between 2Ø and 3Ø (2Ø and 3Ø included)
DELETE Ø,7Ø   deletes all lines up to 7Ø (7Ø included)
DELETE 12Ø,32767   deletes all lines from 12Ø onwards (12Ø included)
DELETE 4Ø,4Ø   deletes line 40. This could also be achieved just by typing 40 and pressing RETURN .
BBC User Guide 235

LIST lists a program. (See page 48.)
LIST   lists the entire program
LIST 1Ø   lists line 1Ø only
LIST 4Ø,8Ø   lists lines from 4Ø to 8Ø (4Ø and 8Ø included)
LIST ,5Ø   lists the lines up to 5Ø (5Ø included)
LIST 2ØØ,   lists the lines after 2ØØ (2ØØ is included).
BBC User Guide 288

LISTO is used for setting out a listed program.
BBC User Guide 290

LOAD loads a program from a cassette or disc.
LOAD "WATER"   will load a program called WATER.
BBC User Guide 292

NEW sets up the computer for a new program to be typed in (it removes any existing program). (See page 50.)
BBC User Guide 304

OLD recovers a program after NEW has been typed in, provided that no new lines have been written. (It can also recover after BREAK has been pressed.)
BBC User Guide 307

RENUMBER renumbers the lines of a program.
RENUMBER gives 1Ø,2Ø,3Ø, ... etc .
RENUMBER 63   gives 63,73,83 . . . . etc.
RENUMBER 4Ø,4   gives 4Ø,44,48 . . . . etc.
BBC User Guide 335

SAVE saves a program onto a cassette or disc.
SAVE "MISSILE" saves a program and entitles it
MISSILE. **BBC User Guide 344**

Statements

CHAIN loads and runs a program from a cassette or disc.
CHAIN "EXACT" loads and runs the program called
EXACT. **BBC User Guide 216**

CLEAR clears all the variables written in a program.
BBC User Guide 218

CLG clears any graphics on the screen, and moves the
graphics cursor to the bottom left-hand corner of the
screen. **BBC User Guide 220**

CLS clears any text on the screen and moves cursor to the
top left-hand corner of the screen. (See page 47.)
BBC User Guide 221

COLOUR selects the colour displayed on the screen. (See
page 43.)
COLOUR Ø to 15 for foreground.
COLOUR 128 to 143 for background (operates in MODE 5)
MODE 5
COLOUR 3
COLOUR 129
displays white characters on red background.
BBC User Guide 222

DATA is used with READ to supply data for a program.
(See page 62.)
DATA 1,2,3,4,5
DATA apple,banana,carrot,date. **BBC User Guide 227**

DEF is used to define a procedure or function.
BBC User Guide 230

DIM allows groups of words or numbers to be put into the
computer.
DIM X(2Ø) allows numbers to be put into the computer
with addresses X(1),X(2),X(3) ... up to X(2Ø). In order to
understand this statement you should read chapter 21
starting on page 120 of the *BBC User Guide*.
BBC User Guide 236

85

DRAW draws a line on screen. (See page 39.)
DRAW 2ØØ,3ØØ draws a line to the point 2ØØ,3ØØ from
Ø,Ø. Any further instruction draws a line from 2ØØ,3ØØ
to next point. The first number, 2ØØ gives the distance
across the screen (along the X axis) and the second
number, 3ØØ gives the distance up (along the Y axis).
(DRAW operates in MODE 4 and MODE 5.)
Ø,Ø is the bottom left-hand corner, and the X axis can take
values from Ø to 1279, and the Y axis can take values from
Ø to 1Ø23. **BBC User Guide 23!**

ELSE used with IF and THEN. (See page 64.)
IF ans=4 THEN PRINT "correct" ELSE PRINT "try
again". **BBC User Guide 24**

END tells the computer that the program has reached the
end. **BBC User Guide 24!**

ENDPROC tells the computer that the program has
reached the end of a procedure definition.
BBC User Guide 24!

FN is used with DEF to define a function.
BBC User Guide 25!

FOR is used with TO and NEXT to repeat the same lines
many times. (See page 61.)
FOR X=Ø to 1Ø:NEXT X
gives X the values Ø,1,2 . . . . . 1Ø taken in order.
BBC User Guide 26!

GCOL is used to select a colour for graphics.
1Ø MODE 5
2Ø GCOL Ø,1
3Ø DRAW 1ØØØ,1ØØØ
draws a sloping red line

1Ø MODE 5
2Ø GCOL Ø,2
3Ø DRAW 1ØØØ,1ØØØ
draws a sloping yellow line. **BBC User Guide 26!**

GOSUB is a program instruction to go to a subroutine
which starts at a given line number.
GOSUB 55Ø instructs the program to go to a subroutine
which starts at line number 55Ø. RETURN is used at the
end of the subroutine. **BBC User Guide 26!**

GOTO is a program instruction to GOTO a specific line number. (See page 66.)
GOTO 41Ø instructs the program to go to line 41Ø.

BBC User Guide 268

IF is used with THEN (and maybe ELSE). (See page 64.)
IF A$="good" THEN GOTO 6ØØ. **BBC User Guide 272**

INPUT allows words or numbers to be put into the computer. (See page 55.)
INPUT A   (for numbers)
INPUT A$ (for words).　　　　　**BBC User Guide 277**

LET is used to give a value or word. (See page 53.)
LET A=8   (for numbers)
LET A$="CAT"   (for words).　　　**BBC User Guide 287**

MODE is used to select screen graphics. (See page 39.)
MODE 5   gives up to 4 colours in the display, 2Ø characters per line, 32 lines on the screen.

BBC User Guide 301

MOVE moves the cursor to a point on the screen with no output on the screen. (See page 41.)
MOVE 7Ø,4Ø   would move the cursor to 7Ø,4Ø. The first number, 7Ø gives the distance across the screen, and the second number, 4Ø gives the distance up. (MOVE operates in MODE 4 and MODE 5.)　　　**BBC User Guide 303**

NEXT is used with FOR and TO. (See page 61.)

BBC User Guide 305

ON is used for options.
ON X GOTO 1Ø,2Ø,3Ø,4Ø   if X=1 the program goes to 1Ø if X=2 the program goes to 2Ø etc.
ON X GOSUB 1ØØ,2ØØ,3ØØ   operates in the same way.　　　　　　　　**BBC User Guide 308**

PLOT is used to draw a point, line, or triangle.
PLOT 69,12ØØ,4ØØ   draws a point on the right-hand side of the screen.
PLOT 5,Ø,8ØØ   will then draw a line from the point to the left-hand side of the screen.
PLOT 85,Ø,Ø   will then colour in a large triangle on the screen.　　　　　　　**BBC User Guide 319**

PRINT Numbers can be printed using PRINT 5.
Words can be printed using PRINT "alphabet". (See page 25.)

PRINT 5,6   gives 5   6
PRINT 5;6   gives 56
PRINT 5'6   gives 5
                        6   **BBC User Guide 324**

PROC is used with DEF to define a procedure.
                                        BBC User Guide 329

READ is used with DATA to read information. (See page 6:
1Ø READ A$,B$,C$,D$,E$
2Ø DATA red,green,orange,blue,pink
3Ø PRINT B$
prints 'green'.   **BBC User Guide 332**

REM is used for putting a comment or REMark into a program. The computer ignores any writing following REM.
REM set the timer.   **BBC User Guide 334**

REPEAT is used with UNTIL to make the computer repeat a set of instructions until a certain condition is met.
(See page 63.)   **BBC User Guide 337**

RESTORE resets the data pointer. **BBC User Guide 339**

RETURN is used with GOSUB in order to RETURN to the main body of a program.   **BBC User Guide 340**

RUN asks the computer to RUN through a program. (See page 50.)   **BBC User Guide 343**

SOUND is used to play a note. (See page 44.)
SOUND I,V,P,T
I instrument 1 to 3
V volume Ø to −15
P pitch Ø to 255
T time Ø to 254   **BBC User Guide 347**

STEP is used with FOR and TO. (See page 61.)
FOR....TO....STEP.
FOR X=1 TO 11 STEP 2   gives X the values 1,3,5,7,9,11.
                                        BBC User Guide 356

STOP ends the running of a program.
                                        BBC User Guide 357

THEN is used with IF (and maybe with ELSE). (See page 64.)
IF ... THEN.
IF X=1Ø THEN GOTO 6ØØ   **BBC User Guide 363**

TO is used with FOR and NEXT. (See page 61.)
                                BBC User Guide 365

TRACE makes the computer print out the line number of each line that it comes to as a program is running.
TRACE ON followed by TRACE 3ØØ traces the output of lines up to 3ØØ. To turn off use TRACE OFF.
                                BBC User Guide 367

UNTIL is used with REPEAT. (See page 63.)
REPEAT ...... UNTIL   **BBC User Guide 370**

VDU is a complicated statement which carries out different functions according to the number following it.
VDU 3Ø   moves cursor to top left-hand corner
VDU 7   gives a short bleep
VDU 12   clears the screen.   **BBC User Guide 373**

Number functions

ABS gives the positive value of a number.
PRINT ABS(−7)   gives 7.   **BBC User Guide 200**

FALSE returns a value of Ø.   **BBC User Guide 257**

INT gives the integer (or whole number) part of a number.
INT 45.61   gives 45.
INT −17.22   gives −18.   **BBC User Guide 282**

MOD gives the remainder after division.
PRINT 11 MOD 4 gives 3
PRINT 14 MOD 3 gives 2.   **BBC User Guide 299**

PI is a constant value PI=3.14159265. The circumference of a circle of radius r is 2*PI*r.   **BBC User Guide 318**

POINT gives the colour of a point on the screen display.
                                BBC User Guide 322

POS gives the position of the cursor across the screen (Ø-left to 79-right).   **BBC User Guide 323**

RND gives a random number. (See page 59.)
PRINT RND(1Ø) gives a number at random in the range 1 to 1Ø.
An example of a program using RND is

```
1Ø CLS
2Ø LET X=RND(4Ø)
3Ø LET Y=RND(24)
4Ø PRINT TAB(X,Y)"*"
5Ø REPEAT
6Ø INPUT GX
7Ø INPUT GY
8Ø PRINT TAB(GX,GY)"O"
9Ø UNTIL GX=X and GY=Y
1ØØ PRINT "SPOT ON"
```
BBC User Guide 34:

SGN gives the sign of a number.
1 for postive
−1 for negative
Ø for zero   **BBC User Guide 34:**

SPC prints a number of spaces on the screen.
PRINT SPC(2Ø);4   prints 2Ø spaces before the 4.
Try the following
PRINT SPC(Ø)"LEFT"
PRINT SPC(17)"MIDDLE"
PRINT SPC(35)"RIGHT"   **BBC User Guide 35:**

SQR gives the square root of a number.
PRINT SQR(16)   prints 4   **BBC User Guide 35:**

TAB can only be used with PRINT and INPUT. (See page 52.)
TAB(9)   will print spaces up to the 9th column.
TAB(12,2Ø)   will move the cursor to the position 12,2Ø on the screen (12th column, 2Øth row) (all based on an origin Ø,Ø in the top left hand corner).   **BBC User Guide 36(**

TIME gives time in 1ØØths of a second.
PRINT TIME/1ØØ   gives the number of seconds the computer has been switched on.   **BBC User Guide 364**

TRUE if a statement is true the computer prints out −1.
PRINT 9=9 followed by RETURN   prints −1.
                                BBC User Guide 369

VPOS gives the row on which the cursor is placed.
                                BBC User Guide 375

Waiter, I'll have C$, P$ and A$, with a double helping of G$ and custard to follow.

Word functions

GET$ waits for a key to be pressed and stores the letter or symbol.
1Ø IF GET$=Y THEN GOTO 3Ø
2Ø GOTO 1Ø
3Ø PRINT "You typed 'Y'"
This program will only go to line 3Ø when you type Y.
BBC User Guide 264

INKEY$ waits for a key to be pressed for a specified time.
X$=INKEY$(5ØØ)   waits 5 seconds for a key to be pressed and stores the letter or symbol in X$.
BBC User Guide 276

INSTR searches a string (a series of characters).
X=INSTR(A$,B$)   looks for position of B$ in A$ and stores it in X.
X=INSTR(A$,B$,Q)   looks for position of B$ in A$, and starts the search at Q
PRINT INSTR("CAMPBELL","M")   would print 3.
PRINT INSTR("CENTRE","E",3)   would print 6.
BBC User Guide 280

LEFT$ copies the left hand part of a word. (See page 59.)
1Ø A$="FELLOW"
2Ø PRINT LEFT$(A$,4)
prints FELL.
BBC User Guide 283

LEN gives the number of characters in a word.
10 K=LEN("BEAUMONT")
20 PRINT K
would print 8. **BBC User Guide 285**

MID$ copies the middle part of a word. (See page 59.)
10 D$='TRIPLET"
20 PRINT MID$(D$,2,3)
would print RIP. **BBC User Guide 298**

RIGHT$ gives the right hand part of a word. (See page 59.)
10 H$="CRUMPET"
20 PRINT RIGHT$(H$,3)
would print PET. **BBC User Guide 341**

STR$ converts a number into a string form.
STR$(46) would give "46". **BBC User Guide 358**

STRING$ repeats a word a given number of times.
PRINT STRING$(4,"Horse") will print HorseHorseHorseHor
BBC User Guide 359

Operators

AND is used to check whether two conditions hold. (See page 68.)
IF sunshine=TRUE AND rain=TRUE THEN PRINT "Look for a rainbow"   tells you to look for a rainbow if it is raining and the sun is shining.   **BBC User Guide 205**

DIV gives the answer when the number before it is divided by the number after, ignoring any remainder.
16 DIV 5   gives 3.   **BBC User Guide 238**

EOR is used to check whether one or another condition holds (but not both).
IF person1=girl EOR person2=girl THEN PRINT "marriage allowed".   **BBC User Guide 250**

NOT is a statement used with IF and THEN to test if something is not true.
IF NOT A=2 THEN PRINT "no"   will print 'no' if A does not equal 2.   **BBC User Guide 306**

OR is used to check whether one or another condition holds. (See page 70.)
IF A=3 OR B=6 THEN PRINT "yes"   will print 'yes' if either A=3 or B=6 (or both A=3 and B=6).
                              BBC User Guide 316

Geometric functions

ACS gives the angle whose cosine is known (in radians), that is arc-cosine.   **BBC User Guide 2**

ASN gives the angle whose sine is known (in radians), that is arc-sine.   **BBC User Guide 20**

ATN gives the angle whose tangent is known (in radians), that is, arc-tan.   **BBC User Guide 21**

COS gives the cosine of an angle (the angle must be stated in radians).   **BBC User Guide 22**

DEG converts angles from radians into degrees.   **BBC User Guide 23**

EXP gives e (2.7183) to any power.   **BBC User Guide 25**

LN gives logarithms of numbers to base e (2.7183).   **BBC User Guide 29**

LOG gives logarithms of numbers to base 1Ø.   **BBC User Guide 29**

RAD converts angles from degrees into radians.   **BBC User Guide 33**

SIN gives the sine of an angle (the angle must be stated in radians).   **BBC User Guide 34**

TAN gives the tangent of an angle (the angle must be stated in radians).   **BBC User Guide 36**